THE DREAMLIGHT LUCIDITY

LUTHER MAYFIELD

Fever Garden Publishing

While every precaution has been taken in the preparation of this book, the publisher assumes no responsibility for errors or omissions, or for damages resulting from the use of the information contained herein.

THE DREAMLIGHT LUCIDITY

Isbn: 978-1-950021-99-4

Second edition. May 3, 2018.

Copyright © 2018 Luther Mayfield.

Written by Luther Mayfield.

❦ Created with Vellum

Dedicated to Jessica

Contents

A Dream Beneath the Rhyming Sea	1
Born Alone	2
Ode to Waves	3
Disciple	5
Born in the Pit	6
Brightest Black	7
Tea Cup	8
There's a Log	9
Same Words	11
Dear Singers,	12
Under Blue Covers	13
Golden Iris	14
First Love	15
All Signs	16
Summer of Man	17
Lost Birds	18
Ocean, Wind, Sun	19
Honey Comet	20
Creator	21
A Connection	22
This Poem is Drunk	23
Silence	24
Little Hope, Big Hell	25
Everything	26
Black Bear	27
Marshland	30
Small	31
Suspended	32
Secret Kingdom	33
Course Language	35
Blood over Blood	36
You are Mine	37
Buildup to a Pun	39

Author's note:	41
Upon Waking	43
Tonight	44
Grey Star	45
Old Waves	47
Good Light	48
Blue Marble	49
Painted Turtle	50
Troubled Sleep	51
Morning Glow	53
Whitecap	55
Afterword	57
Also from Fever Garden Publishing	60
About the Author	61

A Dream Beneath the Rhyming Sea

The trail winds rhythmically
Steadily and sheepishly
Led only by its path
And pushed to its singular purpose
Point-to-point
Second hands are railroad ties
Spaced equally apart
Bound unnaturally to stone and soil

The tunnel approaches
The entrance shattered
Bound and re-shattered
Held together by twisting vines
We are pulled close together
Each and every one of us
A barren stone

Follow the tracks down the vines
And into that wild forest beyond
Where planets hang like fruit
Their angelic halos
Sunken halfway down their faces

Pick the apples, plant the seeds
The ties are ladder steps
Climbing the trees
Beyond is an ocean
That no one has seen
Drop into the waves
And sink down beneath
The drip, drip, drip
Of a watercolor dream
Singing for you, singing for me

Born Alone

I found the trick
The treasure
The buried seed
In a lightless land

Let your dreams escape
Let your hope run out ahead of you
And you will be left alone
With your silence and your sight

Time will chew the problems
And strengthen the wine
You'll crawl in the darkness
And break, and stumble, and fall

You will be alone
On the day that you die

Learn to breathe again
Walk again and learn to talk again
You will be alone
On the first day
Of your new life

Ode to Waves

I have a fascination
That rears its crested head
Now and again.
You'll probably see this strange love
Here and there throughout this collection,
And among other things I've done
If you are so inclined to read them.

And that is my love of waves
Caught on video long ago.
There's something about them
That I find wonderful.

Perhaps it's the multitude of the unique.
Each wave is an individual.
Short and fleeting and ever-changing,
It rolls over a lake or pond or ocean
Or river surface, its life paying no heed
To the whims of humanity.

To view it on screen—it is preferably
So old as to be filmed in black and white—
Is to catch a glimpse of the world
Passing by the world that we
Read about in history books.

LUTHER MAYFIELD

Perhaps this wave rolled
At the same time a foreign soldier
Looked up at the stars and longed for home.
Perhaps it crested
As our president sought elusive answers
To hard questions.
Perhaps it hit the shore
At the same time your grandparents
Went about their morning chores
Newly enamored with each other.

Something was happening as this wave passed.
So knit together is the history of the world
That if this wave were to not exist
Then the entire world as we know it would be different.
Every wave gone unobserved is still felt in its passing.

Disciple

There's not a single friend that I've had
That I haven't let drift away
And only a few have come back.
So when I finally find my voice
To tell of Your great love
I'll have not but dry stone
To pour that water
And I have to wonder how long
I'll resent God for putting me here
And love Him
For letting it remain so
Because I hate the pain
And I love to hate
And I love that pain
And I love to say
Brother, sister
"Love your pain
And bleed out your hate"
As if I don't still feel the same

Born in the Pit

Some people
Are born in the pit
In a cage of beasts
At the crack of a whip

They are made to dance
They are built to climb
They go for the throat
They kill to survive

Like a thrashing deer
At the bottom of a hole
Dug deep, deep down
As far as any shovel goes
They want to see you scratch
They want to see you starve
They want to look down
Like a night sky full of
Dead, blinking stars

Brightest Black

"We can be saved"
It is the sound
Of the thrum
Of a wooden bell
A clickity-clack-clack
Hack-hack-hack
Away at it
With an iron-sharpened ax
The bite of reality goes deep
But the spirit bites back
Clackity-click-click-whack
Bells out in front
Rifles on their backs
Hit with a thump
Accented by a splash
"We can be saved"
So we don't fight back
Head to heart
The distance between
Fire spitting arms
Is deep and brilliant
The brightest black

Listen here
Whack-whack-whack
Children
Are
Soldiers
Are
Children
We can always
Always go back
We can be saved
I am still sure of that

Tea Cup

I can see you through the cracks in the window.
Hushed voices with the fire fallen down low.
I saw you break like the morning over first snow.
I'll put you back together.
I'll see you back in this world.

There's a Log

There's a doll
With a wooden face.
Dry tinder waiting to be lit.
"You can sleep here tonight
But let's not make it a habit."

There's a dog
With three legs and half a tail.
If one were interested,
They could count each and every rib.
When I see it
I want every single thing to stop.

There's a law.
It keeps me standing up.
It keeps my hands free of blood.
It keeps me from living
Wherever I want.

There's a really short highway
And everything leads some place,
Everything except the road
That we're all walking on.

There's a well
Whose mouth locks its lips on sleep.
We draw from that psychological cavity
Where pads the feet of that often fleeting
Dreamlight Lucidity.

LUTHER MAYFIELD

There's a log.
And sometimes I just want to be a bug
Living and scrabbling about on the top.
But when I know I have these thoughts,
I know I'm just wishing for the sky to fall.

Same Words

I want to write the same words.
I want to sing the same songs and play the same chords.
They meant something to me then.
They should mean something to me now.
But they're different.

They have lost their paleness
And stretched their shadows.
The same tree at a different time.
A different shade in a lesser light.
The words of my favorite songs are the same,
But sound different when I sing them live.

I want to write the same words.
To just re-record the same songs.
But I forget that they're living things.
Breathing bodies with growing bones.
And when I think that I can make them last,
I only end up turning them to stone.

Dear Singers,

I hear echoes of your voice
From all your songs unsung
As solid as the walls
That they're bouncing off of

They're honey in color and they smell like champagne
I'm steeped in them as the record replays

I never found your eyes in a crowd
Never heard your voice across the table
Nor the way your words were woven
Dim souls behind the veil
Only you in the speakers
Only you singing the words

"Come back to me"

I hear your old voice scratching
On the documentary
Like a vinyl playing
On a summer evening
The trees outside are moaning
In a low-part harmony
They sing along

"Your life will begin when mine will cease
I hope the songs I write remind you of me.
I 'll love you longer than the Earth can keep
Her hands wrapped around our bodies."

Under Blue Covers

Some stare out, the stars out.
Gaze long enough,
It'll suck your heart out.
Back under covers,
To oxygen smother.
Don't turn the lights out.

Are you afraid of the dark?
Have you hung a lie to guard your dreams?
"If I can't see them, they can't see me."
The toys overhead revolve,
To the continuous, spherical song.
"La lala lala lala."
"Pray the lord my light to keep."

Stay blind. We can't find,
Our scale in terms of size or time.
Who knows what could come barreling out of the dark,
Jumping like tree frogs from star to star?
Pull the sky over us, and squeeze the clouds tight.
Call down the hall to oxygen mother.
Please, please don't turn on the night.

Golden Iris

A single planet
Alongside its hazel companion
It is a day in diameter
It is the iris of
A beautiful girl

She lies still in a hospital bed
The cleanest place to die
But she is always alive
She is golden

A gush of bright
Wine from a sleeve
Her life is that of a pomegranate seed
A small burst
For a short amount of time
She is a plume of pollen
Floating over power lines

Her world is a kiss
On a summer evening
A quick dip
In a shallow stream
The life leaks out
Like sand through fingers
A million granules of history

So rock your head back
And let rain sweet tears
Kiss your daughter's glorious life
Be there
And hold her trembling hand
Your golden sunflower petals
Floating over flat lines

First Love

I fell for the naked word
No sounds but the beating heart
No stage but where you are

I stand with the quiet world
No beat from the car stereo
No appeal to the local radio

I broke with breaking down
No song but the gap between
No strings but the ones I'm pulling
In the people that surround me

I drifted from my sweetheart melody
She won't reply to a single letter
Every story: return to sender

One hour set
Ten at the door
Hands to the ceiling
Fist to the floor
Feedback, and a static hum
You'll always be
My first love

All Signs

There is a curved arrow
With a line through it.
In a bike lane
There are a bunch of little ones
With opposing arrows pointed
Diagonally to the
Left and right.
And I am not entirely sure
How to direct myself
To any of these locations.

On my way home
There is one with flashing nodes
That says
"EXTRA PATROLS"
And 50 feet from that
There is a far-larger billboard
For some piss-y light beer.

At the theater.
During the pre-trailer advertisements,
I contemplate buying a plastic wrap
For my waist to make me skinnier
Which makes me feel better about the
Chest-sized drum of cola
Sitting in my lap.

There are signs that say
"Do not lust"
In squiggly black letters
On every pair of breasts in existence
Top buttons popped
To better display the message.

Summer of Man

It is late in the summer.
The lakes are bloated green
And the last of the sunshine
Is being soaked up.

The sun hangs golden
Like an innocent man
With too many mistakes
Placed upon his shoulders.
He is done.

Each cloud has been wrung
Upon every forbidden tree.
The naked pair is restless.

Our friends are turning,
The green long matured.
They droop ripe
From their family trees.

The first cold wind sails in on a mercy.
She cuts shallow
And September bleeds out its swollen ocher.

Our innocence is a soft rot.
I look forward to the fall.

Lost Birds

I read a lot of poetry on the floors
Of libraries and book stores.
As I am browsing,
The names and titles slink off
When I turn away.

These lost poems
That have moved me and touched me
Exist in some deep place.
Along with the songs of long dead songbirds
In ancient and forgotten places.

Ocean, Wind, Sun

I've heard the comparisons
Like an
Ocean
A Wind
A Sun

Are You those Things?
Can You be an
Ocean, a Wind, and a Sun
All
At Once?

The arguments insist:

The sun ignites the wind.

The wind churns up the ocean.

The ocean puts out the sun.

So do I listen to
The crash of the ocean,
The wail of the wind,
Or the scrape of the sun?

Or do I listen to the Whole Song at Once?

Honey Comet

Set upon the backdrop
Of an insect-sharpened wilderness
Are two young and golden
Demi-Gods
Like wet strokes of sun
They glow warmly under cold clouds
And the living, all-consuming hum of
Spindly bloodsuckers

Dry sticks gnarled by the search for light
Are placed in a pile and burned like heretics
We spin around the small dot of embers like a
Turning knob on the back of a musical toy
The chime is soft and slow

In this town we lock more lips than doors
And move to the cathartic crackle of blazing fires
In a bizarre dance of love worship
Offbeat and wild

The feeling was short, but now: endless
Summer love was a rock solid faith
A hard line. And I wonder what I would have thought
If I knew then, that I would see it falter
But nothing can enter those June and August barriers
And nothing can leave
It is a closed ball of wet gold
Hurtling soundlessly and eternally through space

Creator

Wire bones and lots of glue
That's how I'd build man

A Connection

One of my greatest accomplishments
Is the time—while working at a bookstore—I sold a book to
 someone.

They did not come in for this book,
But through our conversation I realized
That the truth held inside this single work of fiction
Might speak into their lives.

If this is the case,
Then they will feel the same things that
I felt when I read it.
And in doing so they will know me
As they know themselves.

This Poem is Drunk

I'll start with a contraction
Similar to the way I entered the world
Commas are stones in my shoe
And colons, well
We all know what colons do
Yes, I started to rhyme but
No, I will not continue
I'm like a 14-year-old
Who just got hammered
And threw up on their
Mother's husband
"Ima ferk wat ever the do I want
An u cant stop me"
(Lol rofl brb gtg#2)

Words are steak
And MLA is that little tin container
That holds those tiny disc-shaped breath mints
Weeeeeee itty bitty
(I always liked MMA better anyway)

Sometimes I just wanna shove words in my face
I wanna engorge myself and poop for like
2 hours straight the next day
Like a big red meat orgy
Like a big, giant, just
Big, fat, fucking buffet
(No, done rhyming)
What was I saying
Oh ye
Man, it's like
WORDS! Ya know?

Silence

I feel it move in color
I see it slide like wind
Stop and stand still
I want to hear what can only be heard
When you let the world in

It's like the blunt of wine
The fumes of scotch
Or cut of moonshine
It stretches across the sky
Blaring songs of far-off sirens
Cut them off
And come alive like the silence

Little Hope, Big Hell

When you spoke to Moses
On the top of Mt. Sinai
Did you mislead him
Or simply change your mind
It calls into question
All that I believed
About your static nature
And the truth of what we read
It has planted fear inside me
But nurtures hope as well
That through persistent prayer
I can convince you
To douse the fires of Hell

Everything

You saw a speck of falling light.
The reflection from a neon sign
Advertising beer and live bait.
It was a camera flash
As it bounced off of
A drop of water,
Capturing you there
In the rain.

On the way home from a movie,
"It's not that far," you said,
After suggesting walking instead of driving,
Knowing full well that it was that far.
Extra time, as if a thing could exist.
Where you get to walk with a stranger
And tell her everything about nothing.

You dated for three weeks.
Nothing happened. Nothing was going to.

Nothing but the moment.
You were laughing before the rain even started,
And now the moment is decades old.

But there it is:
Who you were.
Who she was.
Alone in time as a flash goes off and captures everything
Sending it nowhere. To no one.
Existing alone in perfect communion.

Black Bear

I've always called the black bear
The janitor of the Northwoods.
Solitary and diligent,
He waddles through the trees
Smelling like a big, friendly trash can.
Campsite investigator.
Birdfeeder thief.

He cleans up after me.
This is not why he must die.
I do not know why he must die.
I just know
That something,
Must die.

I enter the place in which he works.
That musky, shuffling janitor.
I frequent it.
I become part of it.

One day I make a mess.
Old food.
Garbage.
Whatever.
It gets the job done.
It is heaped in a pile,
And he arrives soon after.

He is not annoyed at the mess.
He seems pleased.
He will die like he lived:
Cleaning my mess.

LUTHER MAYFIELD

He can kill me.
He has the power.
As much as any man.
More.
But he will not.
Why would he?
Only if he thinks
That I want his mess
For myself.

* * *

The forest ignites
When the pin hits the primer.
Every eye snaps open.
Every ear upturned.
Who will die
—must die—
Next?

The bullet arcs like a father's football
Towards a learning son.
If the simple brain understood the analogy
He may have even tried to catch it.

The Dreamlight Lucidity

He catches it whether he likes it or not.
Through both lungs, and into a rib opposite my position.
Fear is a teetering vase in his eyes.
He runs and huffs and shuffles
And breaks branches and his heart
Pounds-pounds-pounds
Like his feet like his body to the ground.
The vehicle that carries
The death I yearned for
Has arrived.
And its arrival is heralded by
A final groan.
The janitor's 400 pound body
Is unmoving.
A pungent, black mound.

He is a mess on the floor.
I clean him up.

Marshland

Street lamps and neon signs
Are a comfort in the heart of night,
But cities are just fireflies
In the dark and wild
Swamp of the world.

Small

This is small.
The use of an ambiguous pronoun,
Like a sparking tumor.
This is not who I am.
This is what I seek to become.
What fogged variable will I careen off of?
Which unseen trajectory will latch itself to me?
And I to it?

I am the Earth on which I was born
It is a lot,
But it is simple.
It is small.

I see myself metastasizing.
In my dreams I am large as wrath.
My future is soil and I am exploding roots.
An expanding network of wayward planets.

I am the Earth on which I was born,
And I am being born every day.
I am the breath by which I was sparked.
I am dancing lightning.
I am twirling Earth.
I am small.

Suspended

She drops down like a lever falling into place
Pinning her soul to this single time and single space
The cord around her neck is a sincere embrace
You can see it on her face
You can tell by the way she

Swings

Back and forth
To the beat of the drum
The cracks in her porcelain
Like lyrics never thought of
I'm bringing you back to the ledge
That you jumped from
For just another minute
In the warmth of a setting sun

I can feel you every day
I can feel you trying to push your way through
But they've already dug that grave
And they've already filled it with you

They tried to take the breath from you
I'll make another space for you

Secret Kingdom

I try not make my Christianity a secret,
But it's hard not to when Christianity is itself
A kind of secret.
Cloaked in the smoke of a million opposing opinions.
Stretched thin between wayward points.
A culture appropriated by its own
Confused members.

It's hard not to talk about God,
Without the world talking about God at the same time.
No matter what I say, I speak the actions of someone else.

"In a practical sense,
To follow Jesus is to address your own mortality,
Come to terms with it, take responsibility for the things you do wrong,
And then to follow a path that seeks to do good out of love for mankind
Rather than the fear of death."
(Drink fruit punch and die.)

"Abraham preparing to sacrifice his son
Was a demonstration of the greatest possible sacrifice
For the greatest possible future,
While also foreshadowing the coming of Jesus,
As the sacrificial ram. Simply by showing us to sacrifice ourselves
Rather than those around us, we can make the world a better place."
(God told me to drown my children in the bath tub.)

LUTHER MAYFIELD

"The story of Noah is a macrocosm
Of baptism. Even if one shred of goodness remains
You're life can still be turned around
And the worst parts of you will be washed away."
(God will kill everyone and only leave the believers.)

* * *

The Great Commandment told us to spread
The Good News. Which a lot of people take to mean:
"You will die and burn forever and your flesh will constantly
Regenerate just so it can be seared off again by Hellfire
Unless you say this special prayer and vote Republican."

And it makes me think that
Christianity isn't a secret because of the good things we
    don't say.
It's a secret because of the shitty things we do.

Course Language

Set me on my new course

New vocabulary for new ideas
The stepping stones
Of new believers
As we are called to be
Everyday
We Jump
Hoping to be caught
Lest we fall into
Inarticulation
That ocean with no bottom
And no surface to break

Each letter secured to the next
Cupping the breath inside them
Tiny jars to hold the light
Flickering sounds of our hearts at night

Blood Over Blood

If blood saves blood
When does your commandment
Cease to be about love

If courage and killing
Weren't constantly paired
Could we save our children
Without burying theirs
But it's the sun and the moon, the map of the stars
The image of wrath branded on our hearts

Because I'm a child of God without discipline
We're the crack of skin
From leather whips whistling
Have a child like faith, I've been told
But I'm still afraid of all the things that I don't know
And when your word's at its loudest
I'm still not listening

You are Mine

Another step into
The "real world"
The legs look like legs
Make them like drywall
Make the face gaunt
Like a sick animal
On the edge of death
Then keep it alive
As long as you can
Beat nature
Beat it
Let's have the
Straight line of
Bone
But drawn
With Pencil
No!
A Computer

The
Curves
Were the
Old us, now
We've grown
Into more
We are
"Real"

Skim the fat off
Like a raging beast
Tearing all but bone
From a ripe, sluggish animal
Keep it alive and screaming
Make it walk, fall
Laugh at it
Ha Ha!
Look what we did to you
Look what I did to myself
You skank
You monster
Die foul thing
You're mine
You're mine
The real
World
Is mine

Buildup to a Pun

I made a joke the other day
On a social media page that said
Something along the lines of,
"In an attempt to keep poetry pure,
God made it unprofitable."

Exactly 7 people 'liked' it,
Presumably because any more
Would have been evidence to the contrary.

Perhaps people do in fact dislike
Poetry as much as current sales figures
Seem to indicate.

Perhaps people have grown to hate
The new wave of "Social Media Poetry,"
As I have.
A new trend that incentivizes
Only the most purely Hallmarkian
Of phrases, so as to be palatable to
Your grandmother as she scrolls her newsfeed.
It's abhorrent.
Also, follow me on Instagram.

One must also consider that group of
People that seem to "hate God," and any mention of him.
I very much doubt that I'm followed by a lot of people who
    think that way
But my consumption of Christian media and trash-news
    websites
Leads me to believe that it is at least advantageous to
    use that
As an excuse.

LUTHER MAYFIELD

Finally, it must also be noted that
Not as many people think I'm as funny
As I seem to think I am.
Then again,
That line could just be cover,
The fragile shell that barely protects
My tender insides.
I do admit that, yes
I am quite like an egg.
How?
Well, my friend,
Because I crack myself up.

Author's note:

Finding a place for *Buildup to a Pun*
In this collection was probably the hardest part
Of the entire process from draft-to-publication.

I could have opened with it,
But I foresaw a lot of returns and 1-star reviews.
The act would have been as callous
As telling someone about your horrible
Irritable Bowel Syndrome
And how spicy hot wings
"Gives you the shits,"
On your first date.

I couldn't have ended with it either,
For to do something like that
Would be like being on your deathbed
And telling your child that they're adopted
Right before your eyes close
And the heart monitor
Emits that long and wailing
Beeeeeeeeeep.
"The End."

So here it sits, snuggly in the last third.
Hopefully you're invested by this point,
And *Buildup...* is something akin to
Finally bringing up that tough topic with
A friend who you've earned the right to bullshit with,
Or possibly it's something like that transcendent
State of strangeness one eventually achieves
With their significant other where they can simply
Communicate through bizarre noises and have learned
How to fart in front of one another.

So, dear reader, let *Buildup to a Pun* be that
Pinnacle of intimacy two people can achieve.
Let it be something just between us.
Let it be our weird noises.
Let it be our open flatulence.

Upon Waking

With the Dreamlight Lucidity
Still casting hues on
The projector screen walls
I see the fading shadows of
Imposing figures both frantic and casual
The sound of other people speaking
Using my voice
Ringing phones in my ears

I roll back over
Face half-submerged in the blanket sea
Salt scent lingering
The cleansing wash of waves
Rolling into the end
Of their wild and free lives

I'll remember that feeling tomorrow
Remember the embrace of conjured wraiths
Of projected futures or pasts reanimated

I'll engage in conversation with them
However dead and fleeing

Tonight

"What do you want to do tonight?"
Tonight? Nothing.
I want to sit down
With ceramic eyes
And give a temporary
But definite
Death groan.

All the lines holding
The world together
On a reel
Spinning out.
Colors mix and bleed.
Sound solidifies and
Falls like a lead cloud
Unto the Earth.
There is nothing but the
Steady and gentle hum
Of the generator far
Below my feet
That powers the turning
Of the planet.
Eyes close.
Hold all incoming
Phone calls.

That's what I want to do tonight.

Grey Star

In winter, the forest
Is a stretch of packed white;
Of stunned green and
Spearing amber.

Slow is the step
And fast is the hand.
It wipes away color
And is consistently carving
The fat pine scent
With a silver edge.

I feel her.
Her touch is not physical.
It is a mere presence;
A dab of soft, grey light.

She is a moment.
Every step of the way:
Here she was.
There she'll be.
Never:
Here she is.

The fallen star has four points
Aimed forward and down
An old path.
The hands and feet are synced
-Unlike me-
The space between each is
Long and consistent.

LUTHER MAYFIELD

Welcome.
It is the message
From a carcass recently
Exploded.
Teeth have written
All over the once-blank bones.
The creature's life is gone
And its death is script.

Obvious,
But yet unseen.
Alone, she casts her signs
Of existence into the ether.
Alone I receive them.
But she is already gone.

Old Waves

There are old waves
Skipped across the water,
Or sent tumbling into the universe.
Picked up
By foreign ears,
Or future eyes.
It is the light
Of a sun gone out.
The revolution of stones
Has spun and
Spun and spun and
Spilled like marbles
Into the torrid ocean
Of everything.
They are the forging fathers
Of the children of now.
They are everything
That is now.

But they were once
Just one.
Single.
A wave,
Alone and rolling.

Good Light

The flash is like a splitting tree
And it's splitting me
My glasses are shining up at the ceiling
And I'm shutting down , go down
All the way down and you'll find me there
We don't live at the bottom
But we swing low, we sing slow
We burn our lights long
Until we're pitched in the afterglow
If you're going to catch us
Commit to carry
I'm not entirely sure
That I can hold the good side
Hold too long and the dial slides
From fast to high
From thick to slight
Good night, good light
Good riddance
And good eye

Blue Marble

Snow fell from the sky like grains of sand in an hourglass.
They slowly buried me, my new blanket of false warmth.
Light blue yawned and shifted like a milky marble above me.
The sun like my child's face that I have yet to look upon.
Obscured and flaring as a warning that, I too,
Blaze over another and hide myself in a closing distance.
I heard the trees whisper and groan in the wind,
Like great slumbering friends.
They caught the weight of water upon their many hands,
The perfect white crystals, too heavy for heaven.

Somewhere, in the vast layers of fallen time,
There is a boy like me, staring up,
And the snowflakes fall upon his cold, blue tongue.
They are held there, as if upon one of those tree branches.
The fallen world on praying hands.
His eyes are blue marbles, still and milky.
The sun will warm him only to let him know
That he cannot remain.

Painted Turtle

In the deep blood
Of an endless evening
The river is a lipstick smear
On oil

A line of maroon
That winds along the
Edge of night
Slurring soft
The words of
Dream songs

She pulls me in deep
Further and further
From the charred teeth
Of the shore

She is a tongue of wine
Unspooling and pulling me out

Her lips are dark matter
I sink into a black and red
Watercolor swirl

Troubled Sleep

Backbone of the ugly soul.
There are things no one wants to be shown.
Dreams that accumulate like snow.
All the things no one wants to own.

Between the shaking hands
And pull of sleep,
It's getting hard to care about
Any God-damned thing.
But I'll be damned if they fix me.
So I press my lips tight
And drink deep.

No.
I won't phone-in the fills.
I won't smooth the way.
I won't give up the chills.
I won't ignore the break.

* * *

I'm lighting lamps under glass water.
Searching dead faces in the dark hours.
Their running tears and sharpened cheeks
Are carving canyons into troubled sleep.

The moon burns lopsided in the sky
Like an angry lazy eye.
And the blades of grass are lit with blue fire,
As if each were to guard the way to Eden.

LUTHER MAYFIELD

Stay out.
The night wind shakes
With anger and fear.

Morning Glow

Can you see the sunrise with white eyes?
Can you hear the waves under six feet of earth?
Would you say my name before the drop of time?
After my death and before my birth?

Draw straight lines on cracked stone.
Paint a fire without catching its glow.
Water a garden with blood
And watch what grows.

I am an ever-turning sparrow
Twisting towards the ground.
I don't know where I'll be landing,
But I know how I'll be found.

Could you take my verse
And use it to beat my dead chest,
Put it to my lips and give me breath.
Because I've drawn all these dots,
But still don't know how to connect them.

Whitecap

You are a light
And I am a moth
Colliding like a
Comet and a sun
A quick streak
And a bright spot
Meeting on a
Deep, dark backdrop
Just a wink in a tailspin
A snort in a foxhole
What we are right now
Is gone tomorrow

We die everyday
Churning sand
Sifted slowly away
We are caught under
A blasting
Pulverizing sun
And we are two
Specks of pollen
In a sphere of rain
We are hot and fast
And right now together
Molding, mashing, and mastering
We are one
We are bright, bright
Together
Together at last
I am gone

Whitecap

In the solitary wind
On a planetary grave
Is the force to spark a whitecap
On a brand new wave
We are the feet
On a familiar path
I am sent
A wandering moth
We will come
Together
Again

Afterword

One of my first memories is not a memory of something in the waking world, but a dream.

The dream takes place in a park that is perched at the edge of a steep and rocky cliff. I am sitting there with my mother. The sky is overcast and a strong wind is coursing through the area, bringing with it the rich and cutting scents of the churning water below. The lake is freshwater with no visible shore on the horizon. The waves that cruise endlessly over its surface are huge and white-capped.

This is the entire dream. There is no motion or action except for the rolling of the waves and the ripping sound of the cold wind across the top of the cliff.

A dream analyst or psychologist might say it is the very first visual representation my mind was able to conjure of the play between order and chaos. Order being represented by the well-managed park with its solid stone foundation; chaos being represented by the churning formlessness of the lake below. Then there is my mother, the original mediator between these two worlds. My mother, who brought me from the comfort of her womb into the chaotic unknown of our tumultuous world, ripe with all manner of possibility, whether it be light or dark.

Afterword

The imagery itself was readily available. While it is possible that there is some genetic memory that is handed down through birth and bloodlines, the more likely reason is that I was born in Duluth, MN; a windy harbor city built into a hill overlooking the vast expanse of Lake Superior.

But regardless of the reason for the dream and the meaning that underpins it, the fact is that this image is one of the original support structures for my perception of the world. In other words, the rough and cool feeling that that dream gives me even to this day has come to define my artistic taste and sensibilities and in exploring this dream and countless others, I feel like I can come to better understand myself.

Written slowly over the course of five years, *The Dreamlight Lucidity* exists in the tension between the waking world and dreaming one. In it is a wide spectrum of images that have emerged from my subconscious over my three short decades on this Earth and rather than interrogate them for their meanings, I simply filter them through my fingers and out onto the page. Some of the poems are scenes like the one described above while others are simply feelings or even thoughts that have come to me unbidden in the middle of the night, demanding attention and barring the way back into sleep.

As a reader, I hope that these thoughts and images can, in some way, resonate with you. Hopefully, as you made your way through them, there were certain lines and feelings that emerged to serve as points of connection between us. And while I have attempted to filter out any kind of opinion or "message" from this collection, some of the pieces require such things to achieve an articulated form. And in that articulation is where consciousness and creation have their own part to play.

Finally, I'll leave you with the words of someone far greater and wiser than I:

Afterword

> "Your visions will become clear only when you can look into your own heart. Who looks outside, dreams; who looks inside, awakes."
>
> — C.G. Jung

With great love,

Luther Mayfield

P.S.

One of the funniest things I've heard in recent memory was from an acquaintance who said something along the lines of this:

> "So I began reading *The Turn of the Screw* by Henry James this weekend. I got about two pages into the preface and thought to myself *'I'm not going to read this book, am I?'*"

Having had the same experience with a number of other books, I laughed pretty hard at that. How many times have I failed to even begin a book because of the sheer amount of labor it took to read a preface or foreword? Sure, I could skip it, but what if there's some sort of pertinent information I need to grasp the core concept of the text?

Anyway, that's why I chose this little explanation of the history of this collection to exist at the end rather than the beginning. It's not that I don't think the information here is worthwhile, but by placing it at the end of the book rather than the beginning, I'm signaling to the reader that it is in fact, okay to skip this little bit of meditation on the nature of dreams.

Also from Fever Garden Publishing

The Omen Tree by Fredrick Niles

Ash Above, Snow Below by Fredrick Niles

About the Author

Luther Mayfield lives in Southeast Minnesota where he bartends and sells other peoples' boardgames. In his free time he writes, collaborates with local artists and musicians, and practices introversion with his wife.

www.ingramcontent.com/pod-product-compliance
Lightning Source LLC
Chambersburg PA
CBHW030133100526
44591CB00009B/634